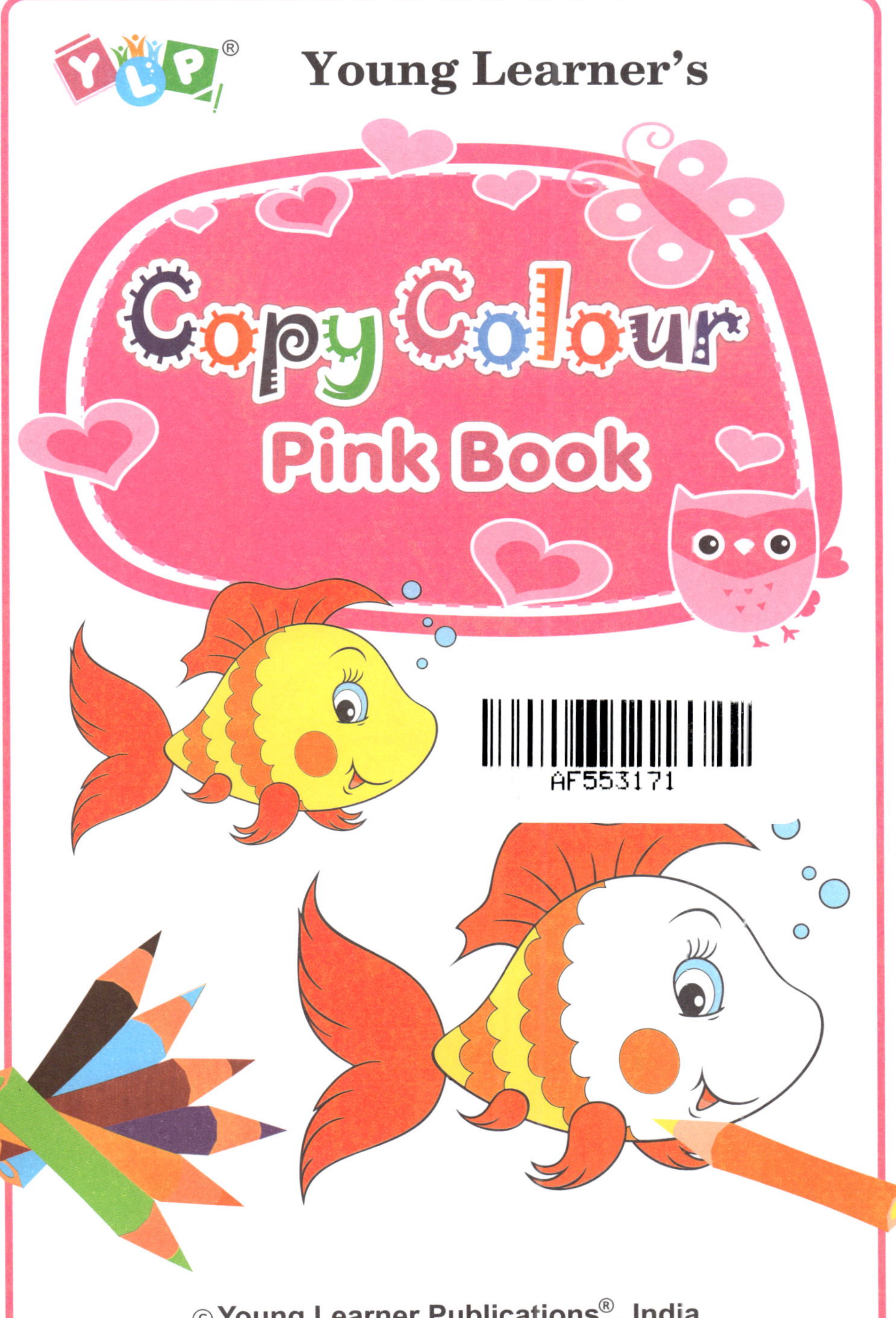
YLP®
Young Learner's
Copy Colour
Pink Book
AF553171
© Young Learner Publications®, India

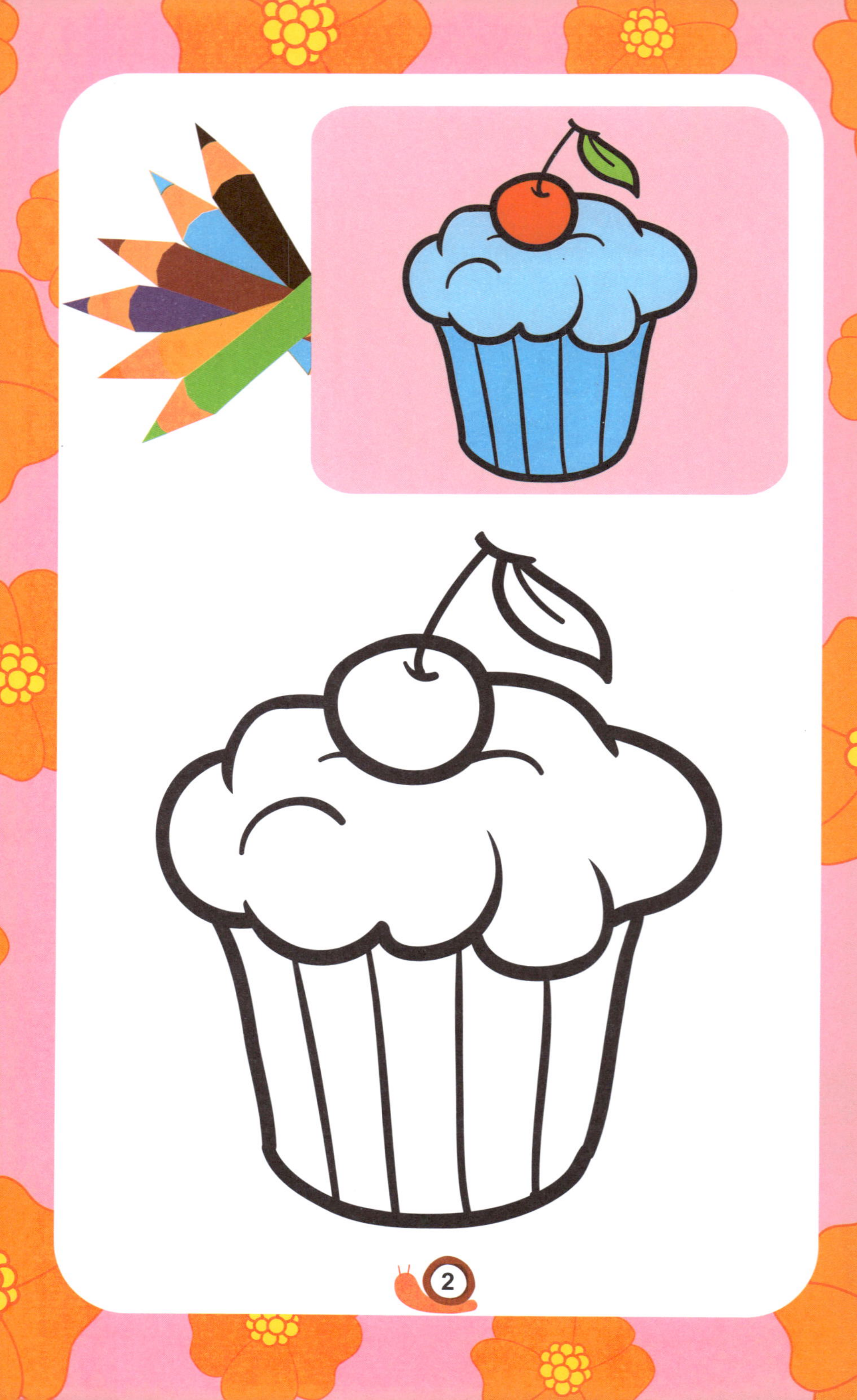

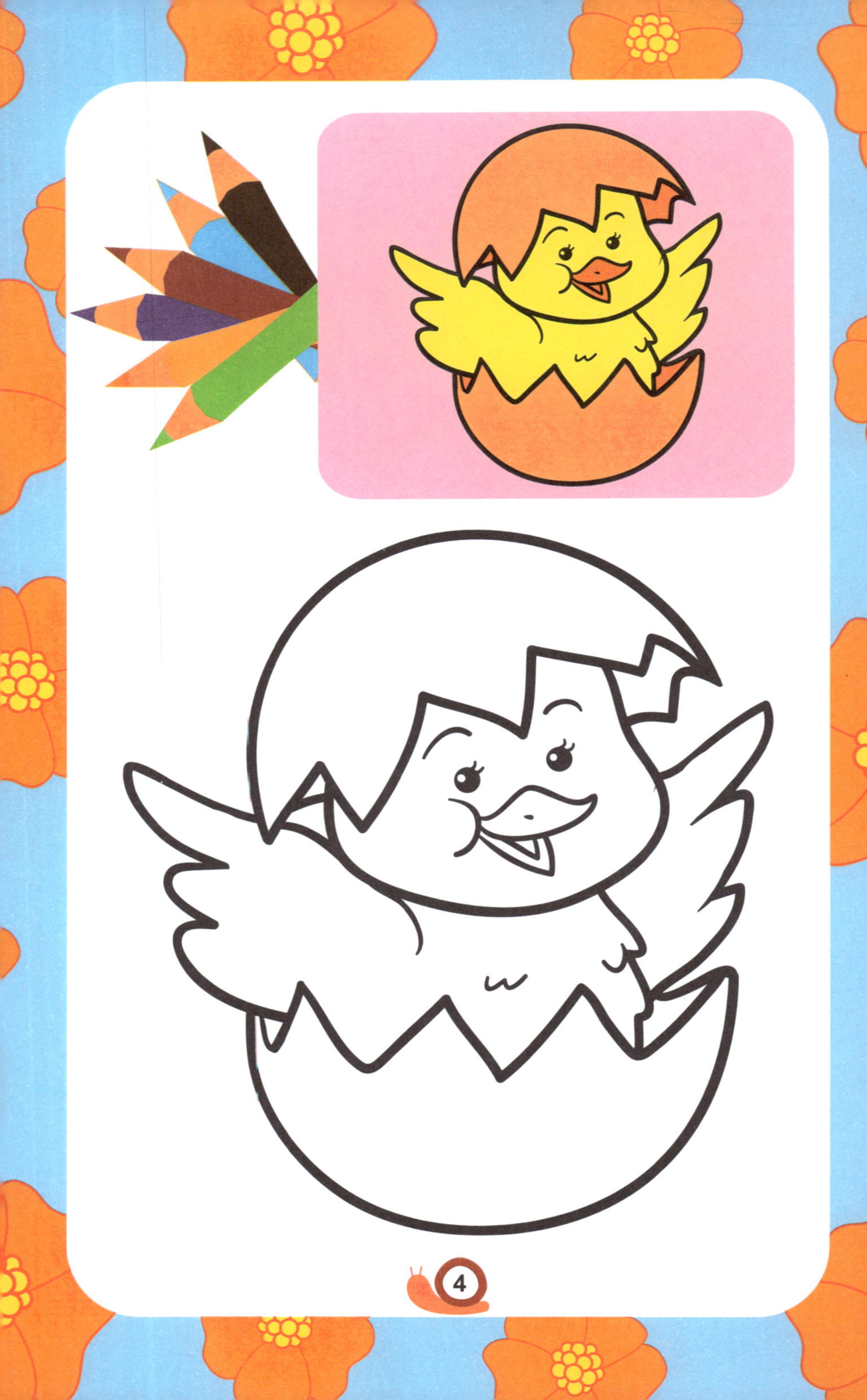

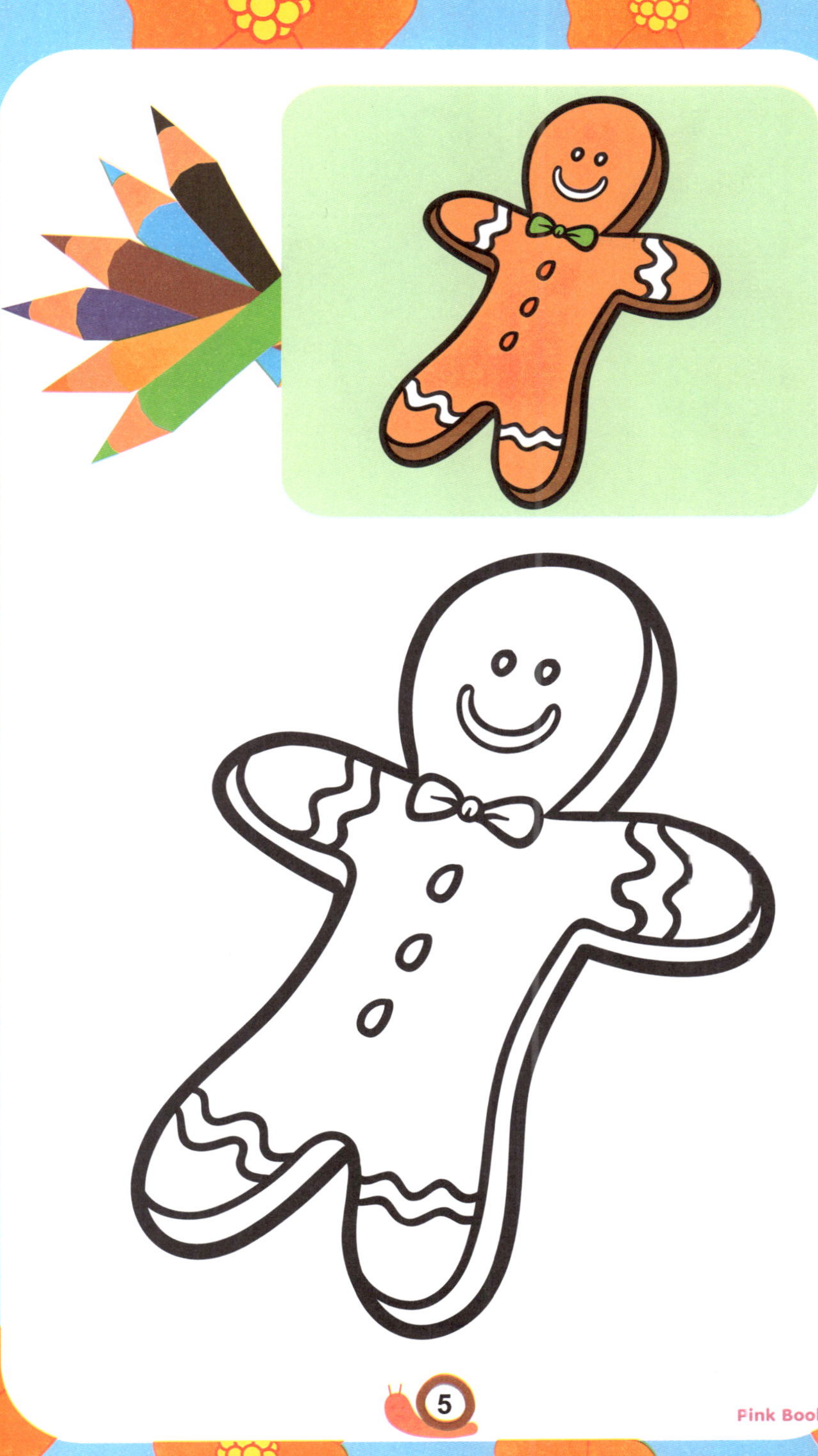

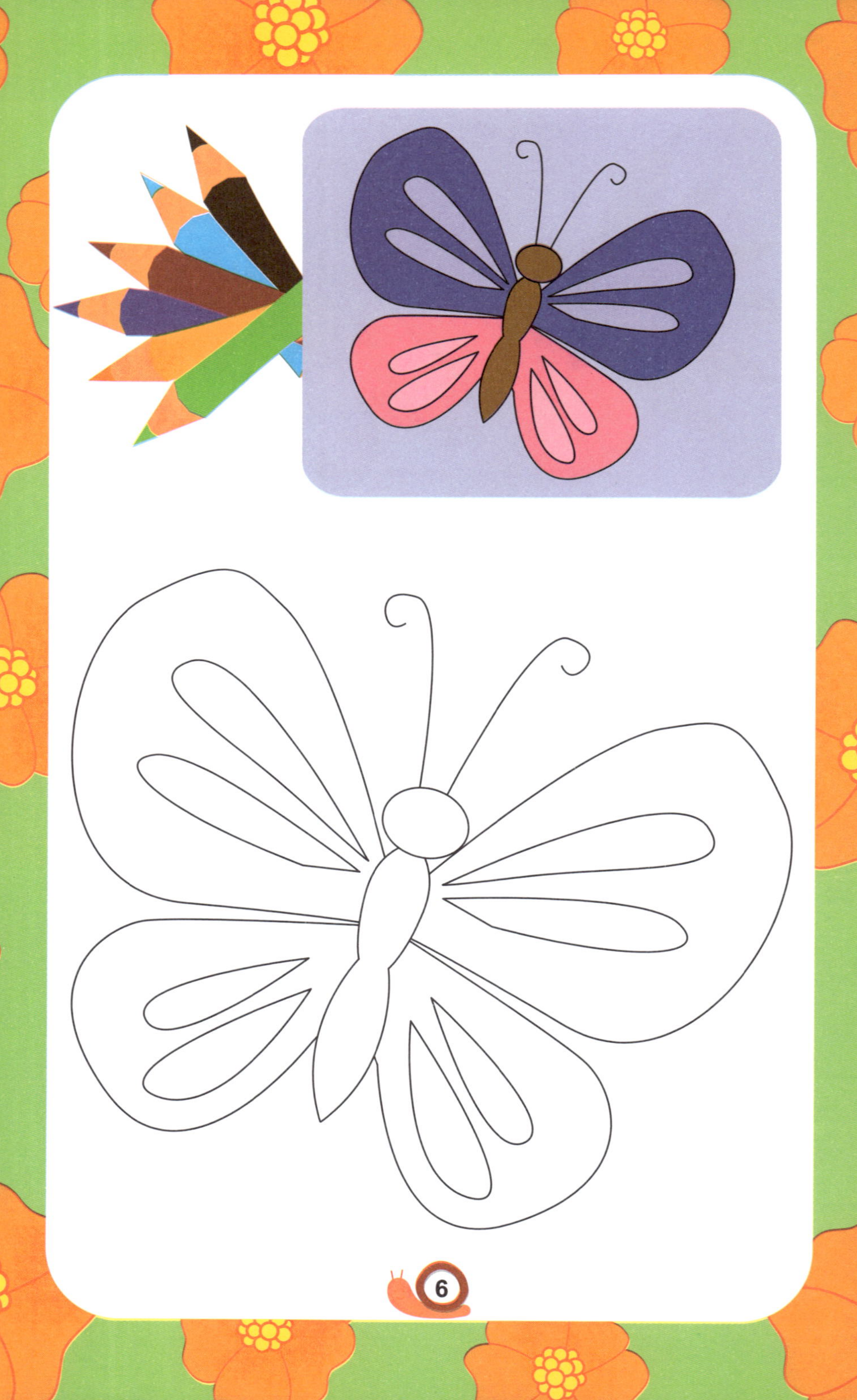

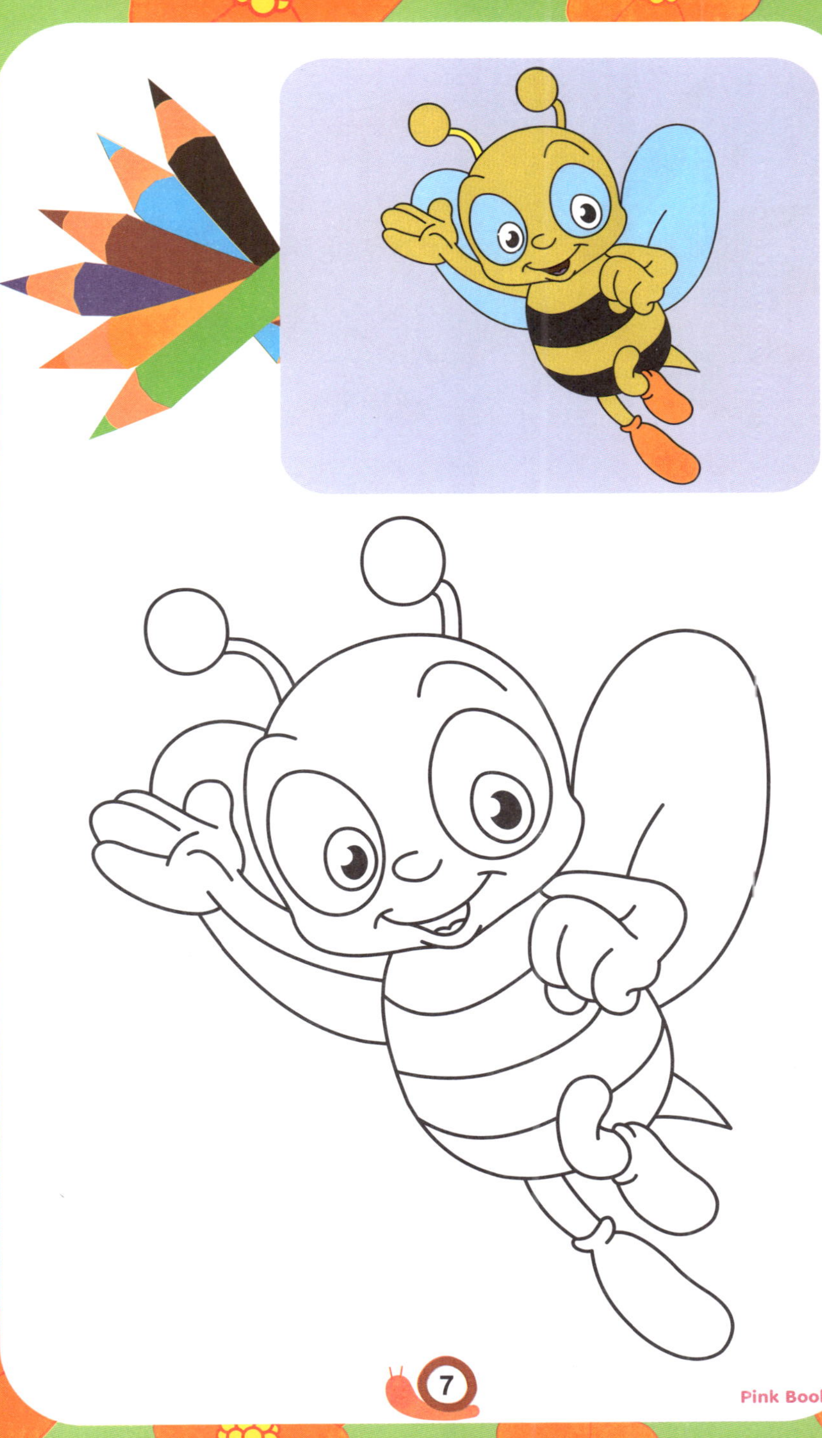

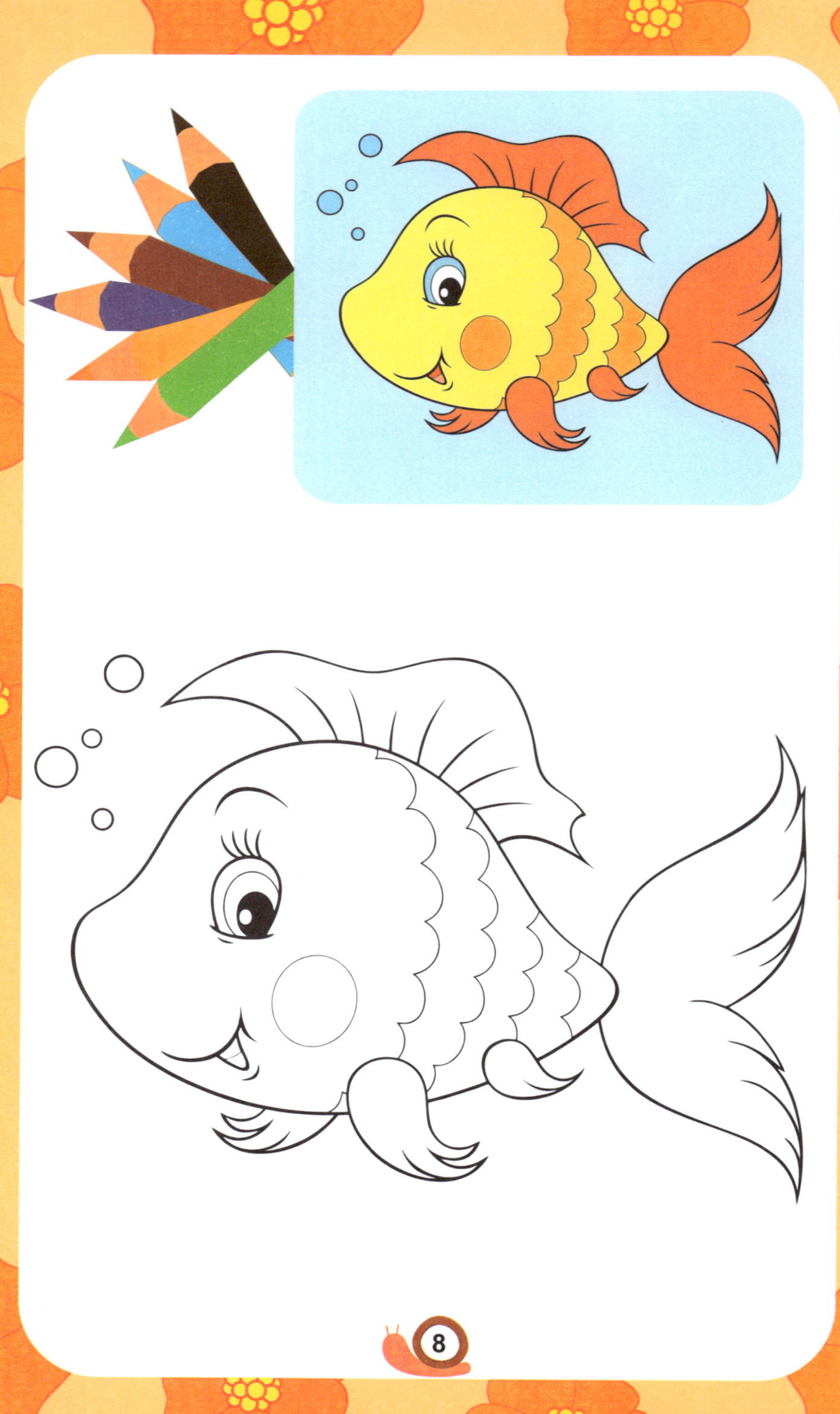

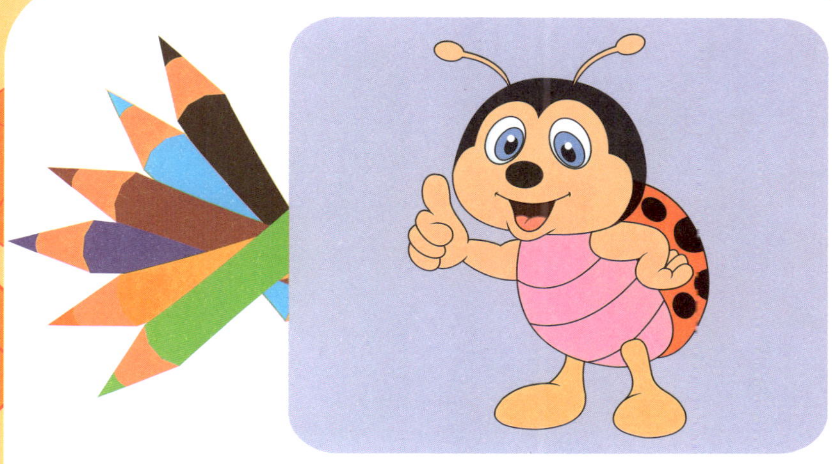

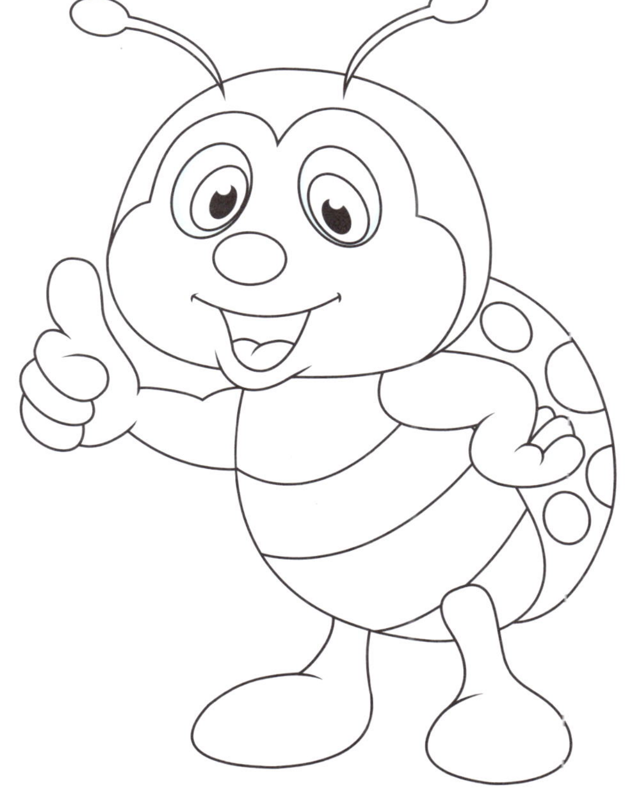

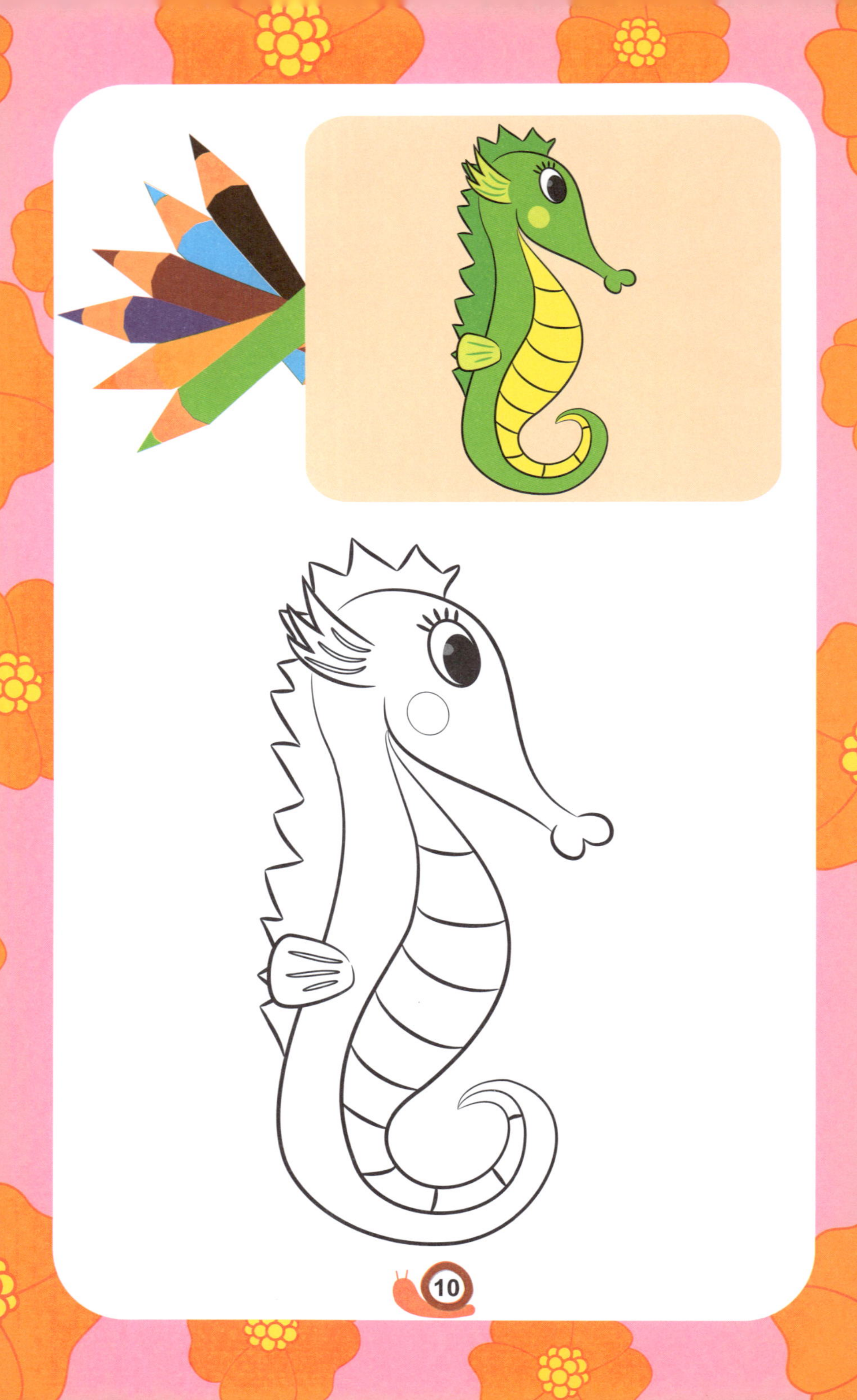

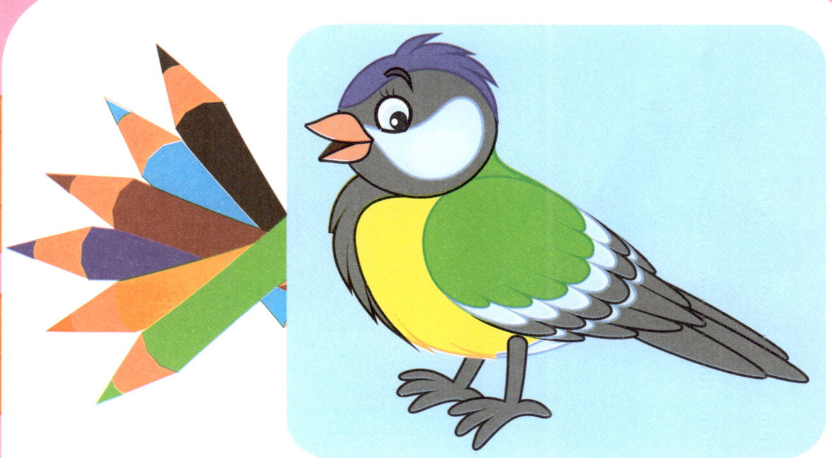

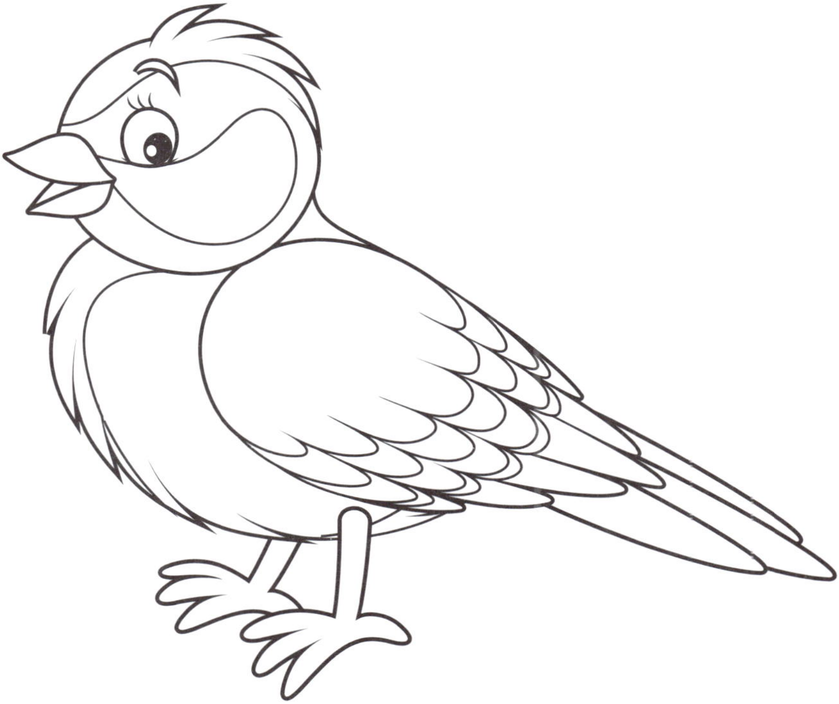

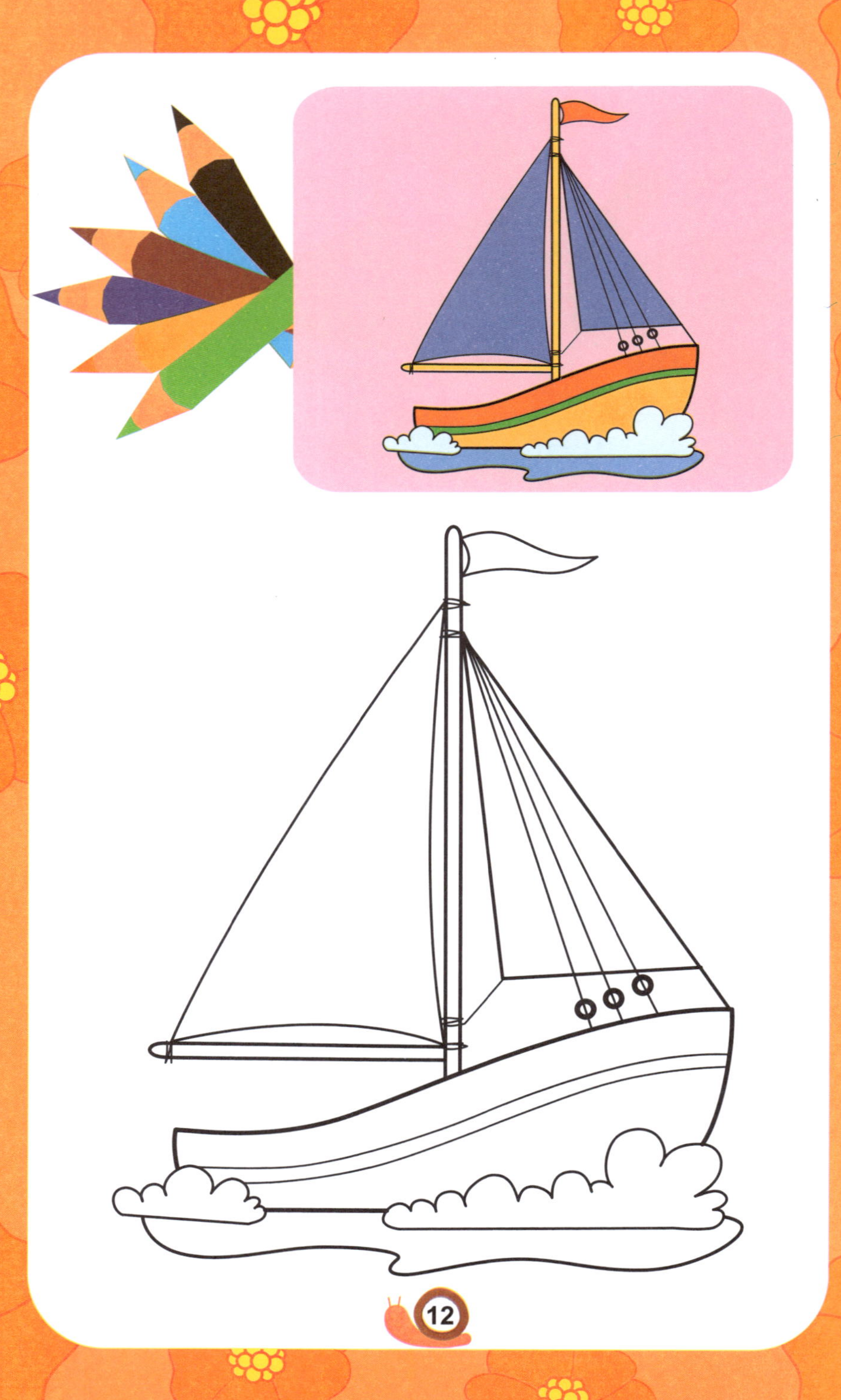

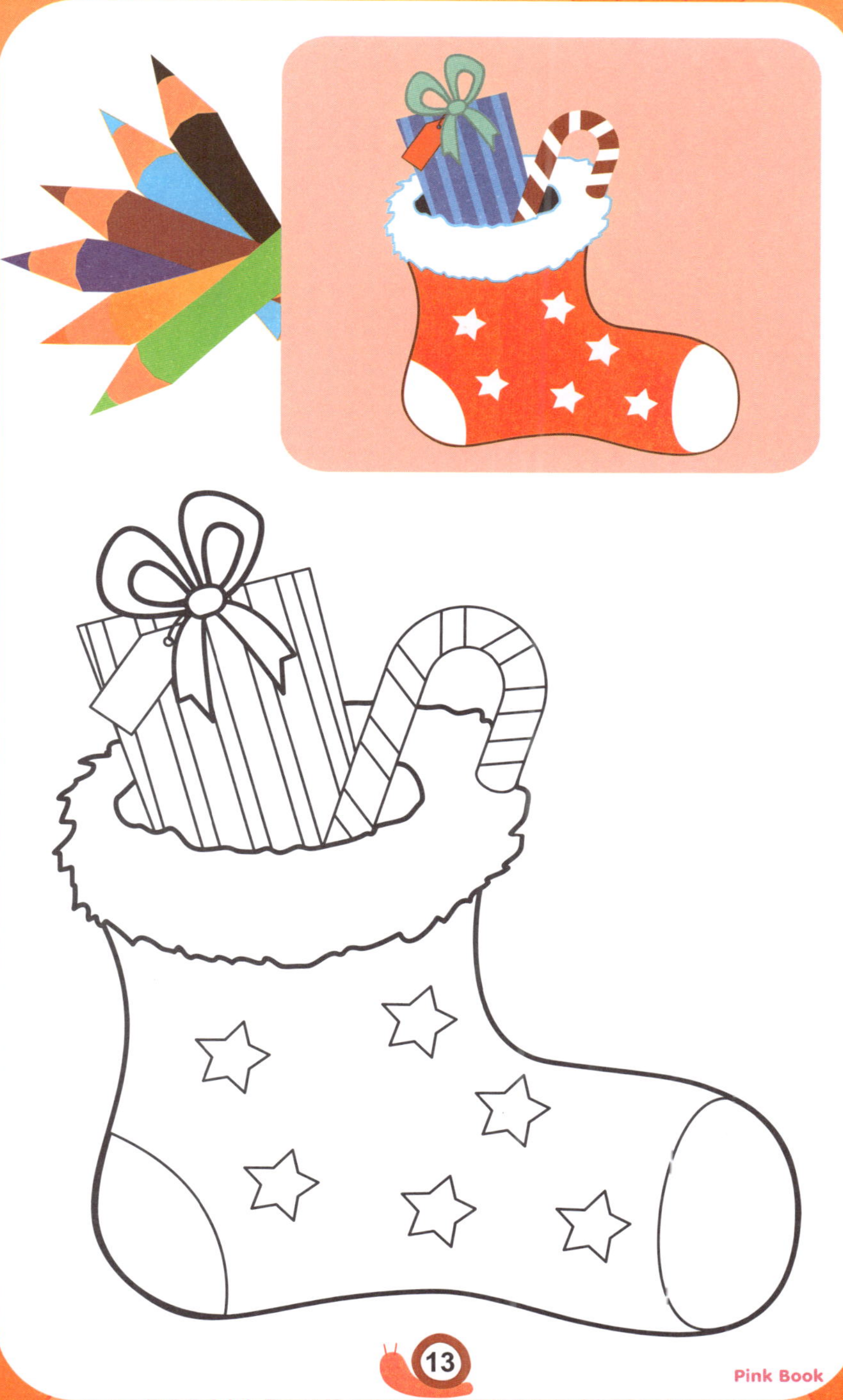

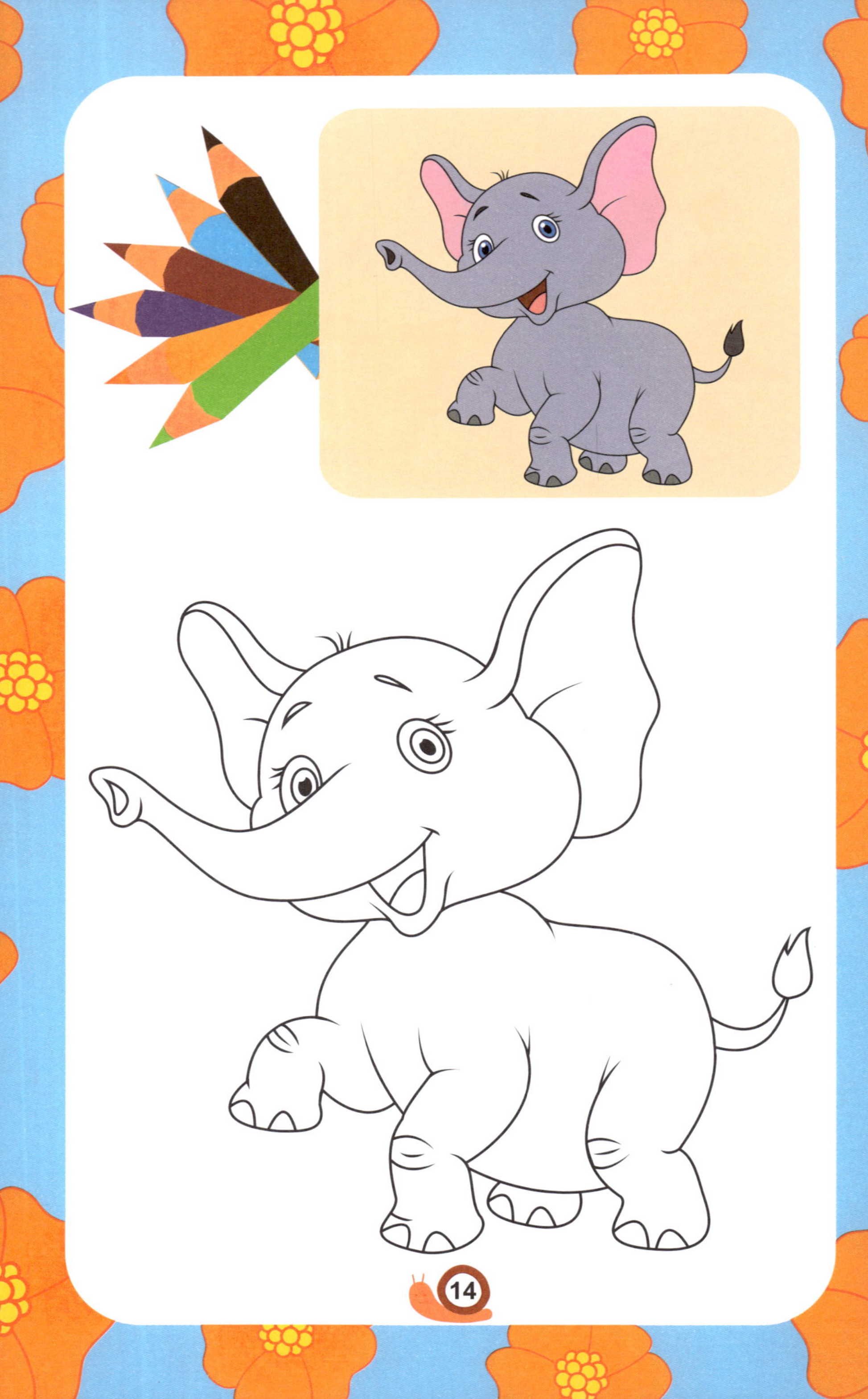

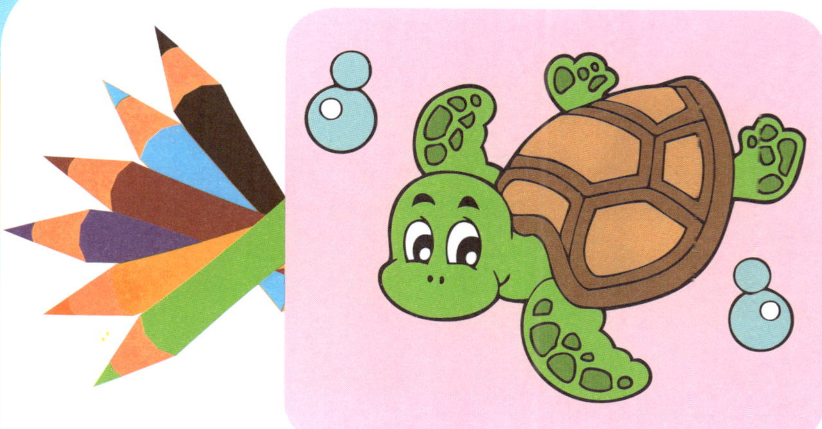

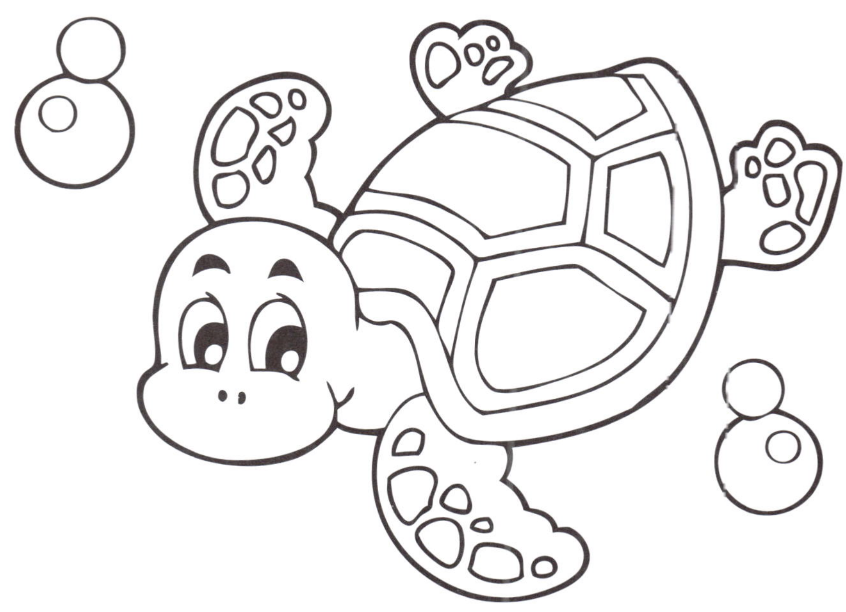

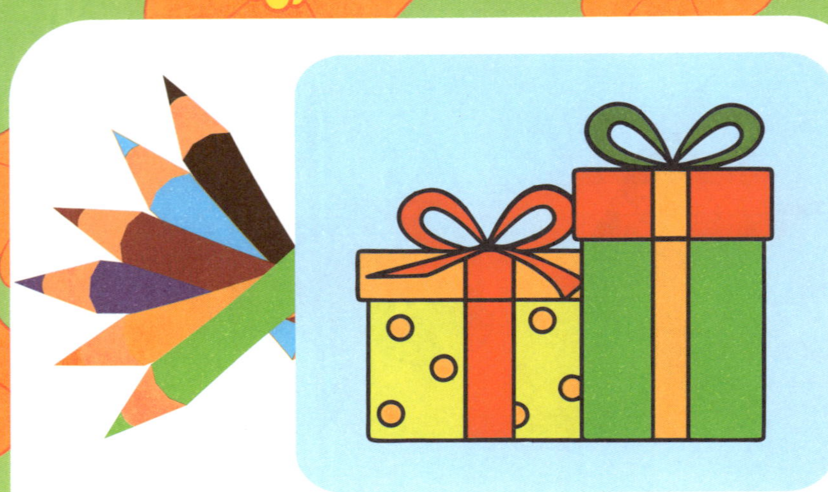

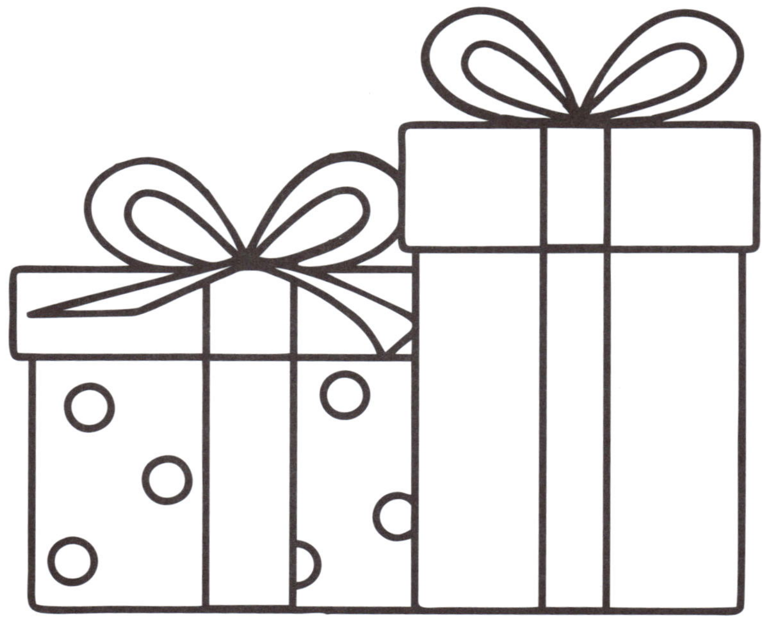